REFLECTIVE EXERCISE BOOK (KEYPOINTS) FOR GEORGE STEPHANOPOULOS'S THE SITUATION ROOM

DISCLAIMER NOTICE:

We Hope You Enjoy Your Reading Experience!

THIS BOOK BELONGS TO:

TABLE OF CONTENTS

Chapter 10: **Future Outlook**
- Preparing for New Threats

Conclusion
- Reflections and Insights

NOTE

Introduction: Inside the Nerve Center

Introduction - Inside the Nerve Center

It feels like you've entered the beating heart of American power when you walk into the Situation Room, where the most important choices are made in a climate of extreme urgency and careful control. The hub of the US government's crisis management and strategic decision-making is the Situation Room, which is frequently veiled in secret and mystery. We explore the complexities of this important venue in this introduction, providing a glimpse into its history, operations, and the significant events that have taken place there.

Formerly the John F. Kennedy Conference Room, the Situation Room is a secure multi-room facility situated in the West Wing basement of the White House. It was created in 1961, during the Kennedy administration, as a result of the need for a consolidated center to handle the Cold War's fast intensifying hostilities. It has developed over the years from a crude command post to an advanced nerve center outfitted with state-of-the-art equipment that permits real-time data processing and worldwide connectivity.

The Situation Room has a sense of purpose and gravity that is immediately apparent upon entering. Screens showcasing satellite imagery, live feeds from multiple intelligence agencies, and real-time updates from global hotspots are mounted on the walls. Every communication equipment and piece of furniture is carefully chosen to guarantee efficiency, security, and functionality. This is more than simply a space; it's a living thing that is always evolving and responding to the state of world affairs.

The Situation Room's primary role is to organize and oversee crisis situations. Here is where the first response is planned, whether it be for a natural disaster, terrorist assault, or geopolitical conflict. The committed group of military commanders, intelligence analysts, and communications professionals that make up the Situation Room staff work nonstop to give the President and senior advisors the most recent intelligence and tactical alternatives. Some of the most important decisions in American history have been taken here, as well as where the President receives the infamous daily intelligence briefings.

Take the 1962 Cuban Missile Crisis as an example of a turning point that demonstrated the Situation Room's critical function. President Kennedy and his advisors spent thirteen terrifying days together in the Situation Room, where they planned their reactions to the Soviet missile installations in Cuba and kept an eye on events. The choices taken in that room not only prevented a possible nuclear war, but they also solidified the Situation Room's position as an essential component of national security.

Let's go back to September 11, 2001, another pivotal event in the history of the Situation Room. The Situation Room served as the focal point for the immediate response as the attacks on the Pentagon and World Trade Center developed. Emergency response teams, intelligence services, and military chiefs were all in close communication with President George W. Bush and his advisors. The Situation Room has a crucial role during national emergencies, as demonstrated by the quick and well-organized actions that were planned from it.

The Situation Room's technological development has been an exciting adventure. Technology has always been at the forefront, from the first days of simple telephones and radios to the sophisticated digital communications, satellite feeds, and secure video conferencing of today. Constructed to manage the most intricate intelligence operations, the contemporary

Situation Room is an incredible feat of engineering. Secure communications guarantee the privacy of conversations, while modern data analytics give decision-makers a complete picture of world events.

But the Situation Room is about more than simply tactics and technology—it's about the people who use it. Prominent personalities such as the President, the National Security Advisor, military chiefs, and numerous more contribute their knowledge, discernment, and frequently, feelings to the discussion. Their choices can have enormous consequences since lives are on the line and countries' futures are on the line. Even though there is a lot of strain and a lot at stake, the human factor gives the Situation Room operations more nuance and complexity.

Another important aspect of the Situation Room's activities is media dynamics. Social media and the 24-hour news cycle have made it possible for knowledge to spread quickly and uncontrollably. It takes careful balancing to manage information flow both internally and externally. Leaks and transparency concerns complicate crisis management by affecting public opinion and having political repercussions. These obstacles must be overcome by the Situation Room in order to preserve operational security while conveying the administration's message in a clear and controlled manner.

The Situation Room decision-making process is always accompanied by ethical quandaries. Leaders are frequently forced to pick between equally unpleasant options while considering the long-term effects of their decisions, the impact on international relations, and the possibility of losing lives. These choices carry a great deal of moral weight, which affects the parties concerned in the long run. Comprehending the ethical aspects of crisis management is vital in order to fully grasp the entirety of the Situation Room's functions.

It is crucial that we consider the lessons that have been learnt from the past as we examine the background and purpose of the Situation Room. Historical failures and achievements provide priceless lessons about what functions well and poorly. Every crisis, from the Cuban Missile Crisis to the 9/11 attacks and beyond, has added to the corpus of information that is currently being used to inform strategies and policies.

The Situation Room is going to encounter new and changing issues in the future. Constant attention and creativity are required due to the development of cybersecurity threats, unconventional warfare, and the unpredictability of global politics. To keep abreast of new threats, the Situation Room must to keep evolving and incorporating new tactics and technologies. This crucial nerve center's continuing significance is defined by striking a delicate balance between looking to the future and learning from the past.

We have barely touched on the surface of what it means to work in the Situation Room in this introduction. We will learn more about its operations, significance, and history as we explore the intricacies and subtleties that make it one of the most significant rooms in the world. We will obtain a profound grasp of the seriousness and intensity of leadership and decision-making in times of crisis through the eyes of people who have been there. Greetings from the Situation Room, the core of global decision-making and the center of American power.

Chapter 1: Origins and Evolution
The Birth of The Situation Room

The geopolitical environment of the early 1960s played a major role in shaping the Situation Room, which is sometimes referred to as the nerve center of US national security. President John F. Kennedy created the chamber in response to the disastrous 1961 Bay of Pigs assault, which was born out of the demands of the Cold War. A crucial weakness in the US national security infrastructure was brought to light during the invasion by the absence of efficient communication and real-time intelligence. Kennedy ordered the creation of a centralized command center inside the White House, able to provide up-to-date intelligence and facilitate quick decision-making, determined to stop such a disaster from happening again.

The original Situation Room was small and contained only a few maps, teletype machines, and telephones for basic communication. A committed group of military officers and intelligence analysts worked there full-time, around-the-clock. Even though it was a simple setup by today's standards, this early effort marked a major advancement in crisis management. The principal aim of the room was to guarantee that the President and his advisors could keep a close eye on worldwide affairs and react promptly and efficiently to any new dangers.

The Situation Room was expanded and upgraded multiple times over the years. More advanced data collection instruments and secure communication connections were installed during the Vietnam War era. The Situation Room had developed into a state-of-the-art operations center during the Reagan administration, furnished with sophisticated computers and satellite feeds.

The necessity for instantaneous, trustworthy information and the growing complexity of world politics drove this transformation.

Additional developments came with the conclusion of the Cold War and the start of the digital era. With the secure video conferencing facilities installed in the Situation Room, the President may hold direct conversations with intelligence chiefs, military chiefs, and international leaders. Making better decisions was made possible by the integration of real-time intelligence streams and satellite imaging, which gave a thorough picture of global hotspots.

The Situation Room has endured as a representation of American tenacity and a proof of the country's dedication to national security throughout its development. It has seen some of the most significant crises in human history resolved, as well as the emergence and collapse of political regimes and the introduction of new technology. From its modest beginnings to its current position as the hub of American crisis management and strategic planning, the interesting history of the Situation Room is chronicled in this chapter.

Chapter 2: Key Figures
Influential Decision Makers

Numerous powerful people have passed through the Situation Room, each leaving their lasting imprint on history. This chapter explores the lives and achievements of the influential figures who affected history from within this crucial area. Some of the most important choices in modern history have been made in the Situation Room, by presidents, their national security advisors, military chiefs, and intelligence chiefs.

We start with President John F. Kennedy, whose foresight and tenacity made the Situation Room possible. Kennedy set the bar for succeeding administrations with his hands-on style and insistence on having access to current information. His command center during the Cuban Missile Crisis, the Situation Room, demonstrated the value of strategic planning and well-informed decision-making.

Next, we look at President Ronald Reagan's contributions, during which the Situation Room's capabilities witnessed tremendous growth. Reagan's resolute efforts throughout the Cold War, especially his calculated attempts to oppose the Soviet Union, highlighted the Situation Room's pivotal role in determining U.S. foreign policy. In order to ensure that the Situation Room could effectively manage the growing demands of the international stage, Colin Powell, Reagan's national security advisor, played a crucial role in streamlining the organization's operations.

During the presidency of George H.W. Bush, the Situation Room in the middle of the Gulf War was observed. The strategic acumen of Bush's advisors and his cool-headed approach to handling diplomatic relations and military operations underscored the significance of the Situation Room in directing multinational coalitions and coordinating military operations. Operation Desert Storm's nerve center was located in this area, which allowed for quick decision-making and real-time updates.

New issues and prominent people came to light in the wake of 9/11. During the immediate aftermath of the attacks and the ensuing War on Terror, President George W. Bush and his team—including Vice President Dick Cheney and National Security Advisor Condoleezza Rice—heavily depended on the Situation Room. Coordinating the reaction to one of the biggest disasters in American history required the room's ability to deliver secure communication and real-time intelligence.

These individuals, among numerous others, had a part in shaping the development of the Situation Room and its significance in US national security. In addition to influencing the course of events, their judgment, leadership, and plans emphasized the Situation Room's crucial role as the center of crisis management and strategic planning.

Chapter 3: Historic Crises
The Cuban Missile Crisis

One of the riskiest periods in modern history is the October 1962 Cuban Missile Crisis, a 13-day standoff that put the world in danger of nuclear war. The Situation Room became the hub of extensive strategic preparation and intensive deliberation for President Kennedy and his aides. This chapter gives a thorough explanation of what happened during the Cuban Missile Crisis and gives readers a behind-the-scenes peek at what went on in the Situation Room.

Just 90 miles off the coast of Florida, Soviet ballistic missile facilities were found by AmericanU-2 observation aircraft, sparking the start of the crisis. Kennedy and his advisors discussed the best course of action in the Situation Room following a series of pressing meetings brought on by this discovery. The stakes were unfathomably high; one wrong move could spark a full-scale nuclear conflict between the US and the USSR.

Kennedy's Executive Committee, or ExCom, met in the Situation Room to evaluate the circumstances and decide on a course of action. The conversations were tense and full of passion. A full-scale invasion of Cuba would come after an urgent airstrike to eliminate the missile installations, according to certain experts, including General Curtis LeMay. Others, such as Attorney General Robert Kennedy and Secretary of Defense Robert McNamara, advised prudence out of concern that such bold measures might spark a Soviet counterattack.

The Situation Room was always busy during the crisis. Updates on Soviet military movements and the condition of the missile systems were provided by the constant stream of intelligence information. Tests were conducted on the room's communication capabilities, which enabled safe connections between the Pentagon, the White House, and US allies across the globe. In order to stop more Soviet shipments of military hardware to Cuba, a naval blockade, or "quarantine," was established. In this regard, the Situation Room was essential to its management.

On October 27, 1962, also referred to as "Black Saturday," when an American U-2 plane was shot down over Cuba, tensions peaked and it appeared as though nuclear war may break out. President Kennedy and his advisors were under intense pressure to reach a peaceful conclusion in the Situation Room. Following lengthy discussions, a deal was reached through covert negotiations between Robert Kennedy and Soviet Ambassador Anatoly Dobrynin: in exchange for publicly pledging not to invade Cuba, the United States would covertly decommission its Jupiter missiles in Turkey, which the Soviet Union considered to be a threat.

The Cuban Missile Crisis was resolved in a way that prevented a nuclear war and proved how crucial the Situation Room is to handling high-stakes emergencies. The experience demonstrated the room's ability to communicate securely and gather intelligence in real time, and it also emphasized the value of making thoughtful decisions under duress. The Situation Room's operations and US national security plans are still influenced by the lessons learnt during this crisis.

Chapter 4: Modern Challenges
The Response to 9/11

For both the United States and the rest of the globe, the terrorist events of September 11, 2001, represented a turning point. The Situation Room served as the command post for the quick handling of an extraordinary crisis on that tragic morning. This chapter gives a detailed overview of the decisions made in real time and the difficulties encountered during and after the 9/11 attacks in the Situation Room.

On September 11, 2001, at 8:46 AM, American Airlines Flight 11 collided with the World Trade Center's North Tower. In a matter of minutes, the Situation Room was a flurry of activity as security and intelligence personnel hurried to determine the extent of the assault. It was evident that the United States was the target of a well-planned terrorist assault at 9:03 AM when United Airlines Flight 175 crashed into the South Tower.

President George W. Bush was alerted immediately and hurried to Air Force One when he was visiting a school in Florida. To handle the problem, Vice President Dick Cheney met in the Situation Room with important advisors. Cheney maintained continuous connection with President Bush, the Federal Aviation Administration (FAA), the Pentagon, and other important agencies because to the room's secure communication capabilities.

The grounding of all civilian airplanes in the United States was a historic decision that had to be made quickly to stop other hijackings, and the Situation Room was instrumental in making this happen. The military's mobilization and the coordination of emergency services' responses in New

York and Washington, D.C. were also facilitated by the room. In the middle of the commotion, the President and his advisors were able to make educated decisions because to the real-time flow of information, which included satellite imagery and intelligence updates.

The Situation Room remained the focal point of the reaction in the days that followed the attacks. The War on Terror was planned and carried out in the room by President Bush and his National Security team, which included Secretary of Defense Donald Rumsfeld and National Security Advisor Condoleezza Rice. Among these was the invasion of Afghanistan with the goal of overthrowing the Taliban and dismantling al-Qaeda.

The need for a strong, adaptable, and responsive national security infrastructure was highlighted by the 9/11 attacks. The Situation Room's crucial significance in handling contemporary operations was demonstrated by its capacity to handle the immediate response and organize ongoing operations.

difficulties. Significant adjustments to the intelligence community's organizational structure and national security policy resulted from the attacks as well; many of these adjustments were planned and overseen from the Situation Room.

Chapter 5: The Role of Advisors Strategic Counsel and Impact

Strategic Counsel and Impacting addition to its technology and infrastructure, the Situation Room's efficacy also depends on the knowledge and advice of the advisors who work within. This chapter examines the crucial role advisers play in the decision-making process, emphasizing their techniques, contributions, and the advice they provides effect on national security.

Advisors on national security, in particular, are crucial. They oversee the coordination of the interagency process and make sure that all pertinent data and viewpoints are taken into account in their capacity as the President's senior advisor on matters of national security. Over their tenure, influential individuals including Condoleezza Rice, Zbigniew Brzezinski, and Henry Kissinger shaped U.S. foreign policy and national security strategy.

Equally important is the involvement of military advisors, such as the Chairman of the Joint Chiefs of Staff. The President receives military choices, capabilities assessments, and strategic recommendations from these advisors. Their distinct perspective based on operational and military experience makes them invaluable during times of crisis.

The President receives vital intelligence assessments and threat analyses from intelligence advisors, which include the Director of National Intelligence (DNI) and the chiefs of agencies like the CIA and NSA. Within the fast-paced Situation Room, their ability to synthesize large amounts of information and give clear, actionable insights is crucial.

The dynamics of the advisory process are also covered in this chapter, along with the difficulties in handling divergent viewpoints and the significance of promoting teamwork. Even in the face of difficulty, advisors must balance conflicting interests, negotiate complicated political environments, and offer straightforward advice. Their support is essential to the Situation Room's effectiveness as well as the country's safety and security.

Chapter 6: Media Dynamics
The Influence of News and Leaks

The media's impact on national security and Situation Room operations is enormous in this day of instant messaging and round-the-clock news cycles. This chapter explores the intricate interaction between the media and the Situation Room, as well as how press coverage, information leaks, and public opinion affect crisis management and decision-making.

Regarding national security, the media has two roles to play. On the one hand, it functions as a channel for information, distributing news and influencing how the general public perceives events. However, it can also be a source of criticism and pressure, affecting how lawmakers respond and how the public views the efficiency of the government. This dynamic must be navigated by the Situation Room, which must strike a balance between the necessity of operational security and transparency.

Information leaks are a serious problem. Unauthorized releases of sensitive data can endanger lives, undermine operations, and harm diplomatic ties. The Situation Room needs to be on the lookout for leaks at all times, enforcing strict security procedures and handling the aftermath when they do happen. Significant incidents like the Edward Snowden and Wikileaks breaches have brought attention to how crucial it is to preserve the confidentiality of classified data.

Public perception is one area in which the media has an impact. The narrative around a crisis can be shaped by news coverage, which can impact political pressure and public opinion. This dynamic must be considered by the Situation Room in order to properly inform the public of its actions and choices. To do this, a concerted effort with the White House Communications Office is needed to design communications that communicate the administration's viewpoint while upholding credibility and confidence.

This chapter explores media dynamics management tactics and issues, with a focus on significant cases from recent history. The interaction between the Situation Room and the media has played a crucial role in determining how crises turn out and how the public views the administration's leadership, from how the Gulf War was handled to how the country responded to the 9/11 attacks.

Chapter 7: Ethical Dilemmas Balancing Morality and Strategy

The demands of national security frequently cause difficult ethical decisions to be made in the Situation Room, where the distinctions between right and evil are muddled. This chapter examines the moral dilemmas that policymakers encounter and how they strike a balance between strategy and morality when pursuing national goals.

There are many different circumstances that can lead to ethical difficulties in the Situation Room. Moral considerations play a major role in decisions about military intervention, covert operations, and the employment of cutting edge surveillance technologies. Leaders have to balance the advantages and disadvantages of their decisions, taking into account both short- and long-term effects.

The choice to employ force presents one of the biggest ethical dilemmas. The intentional taking of human life in military interventions, drone strikes, and targeted murders raises concerns about the morality and proportionality of such acts. The Situation Room has to tread carefully in these moral waters, making sure that choices are supported by both moral and legal principles.

Operations involving intelligence collecting and surveillance may pose ethical challenges. The values of civil liberties and privacy frequently clash with the necessity to safeguard national security. In order to prevent acts made in the name of security from undermining the fundamental principles of democracy and individual liberties, the Situation Room must strike a balance between these conflicting interests.

This chapter looks at particular instances when moral conundrums have surfaced, like the raid that resulted in Osama bin Laden's death, the employment of advanced interrogation methods, and the monitoring systems made public by Edward Snowden. Readers can better understand the moral complexity defining Situation Room operations and the significance of moral leadership in national security by examining these cases.

Chapter 8: Technological Advances Surveillance and Cybersecurity

The capabilities of the Situation Room have changed due to the quick development of technology, making cybersecurity, intelligence collecting, and surveillance activities more efficient. This chapter examines how the Situation Room's activities have been impacted by technology advancements, stressing significant discoveries and their consequences for national security.

With developments in drones, electronic intelligence-gathering instruments, and satellite imagery, surveillance technology has dramatically improved. These technological advancements give the Situation Room unmatched insights into world events and allow for the real-time surveillance of any threats. The ability to analyze and interpret enormous amounts of data has been significantly improved by the integration of artificial intelligence and data analytics, producing actionable intelligence that guides strategic decisions.

An increasingly important area of attention for the Situation Room is cybersecurity. The emergence of cyberthreats, such as ransomware, state-sponsored attacks, and data breaches, presents serious dangers to the security of the country. The Situation Room is responsible for coordinating the defense of vital infrastructure against cyberattacks, development of offensive capabilities to counter and deter cyberthreats, and protection against cyberattacks. Close cooperation with the National Security Agency, the Department of Homeland Security, and other important agencies is required for this.

There are new potential and challenges associated with the use of technology in intelligence gathering and covert operations. The capacity to carry out covert operations and safeguard sensitive data has improved thanks to developments in cryptography, encrypted communication, and biometric identification. These powers must be weighed against the possibility of abuse and ethical issues, though.

This chapter explores the advantages and drawbacks of the technology improvements that have influenced the Situation Room's functioning. Through comprehension of the function of technology in national security, readers acquire a more profound admiration for the competencies and intricacies of the Situation Room in the contemporary period.

Chapter 9: Lessons from History Mistakes and Successes

There have been many successes and disappointments in the Situation Room's history, and each one has taught us important lessons for the future. This chapter looks at significant historical occurrences, evaluating the choices made, the results obtained, and the lessons discovered from both successes and failures.

The value of well-informed decision-making, strategic planning, and efficient communication is demonstrated by achievements like the successful raid on Osama bin Laden's compound and the calm conclusion of the Cuban Missile Crisis. These examples highlight the importance of having access to real-time intelligence, integrating many viewpoints, and being flexible enough to adjust to changing conditions quickly.

On the other hand, mishaps like the invasion of the Bay of Pigs and the intelligence lapses that preceded the 9/11 attacks highlight the risks associated with insufficient preparation, poor coordination, and an excessive dependence on faulty intelligence. These occurrences highlight the vital requirement of thorough risk assessment, rigorous analysis, and a willingness to challenge presumptions and common wisdom.

The function of institutional memory and the significance of drawing lessons from the past are also covered in this chapter. In order to make sure that the lessons of history are not forgotten, The Situation Room has accumulated a body of knowledge that influences present practices and policies. Readers learn about the development of the Situation Room and the ongoing enhancement of its functions by looking at both the achievements and shortcomings of the past.

Chapter 10: Future Outlook Preparing for New Threats

The Situation Room must employ creative thinking and flexible tactics to counter new and emerging dangers as the world around them changes. This chapter examines the Situation Room's future prospects, outlining the difficulties and possibilities that lay ahead.

National security is seriously threatened by new dangers including cyberwarfare, artificial intelligence, and unconventional warfare methods. In order to defend against and address these threats, the Situation Room needs to keep ahead of these advances by utilizing new technology and tactics. Close cooperation with technology specialists, intelligence services, and foreign partners is required for this.

There are additional difficulties brought about by climate change and its effects, which include population dislocation, resource scarcity, and natural disasters. To make sure that the US is ready to handle the security ramifications of climate change, the Situation Room needs to include environmental considerations in its strategic planning.

Geopolitical changes necessitate ongoing attention to detail and flexible approaches, as seen in the advent of new powers and the reappearance of long-standing rivalries. These intricacies must be managed by the Situation Room, which must strike a balance between the necessity of diplomacy and the necessity of defending national interests. This entails building solid coalitions, creating new business ventures, and upholding a stable yet adaptable military posture.

The potential for new technology to improve the Situation Room's capabilities is also covered in this chapter. New avenues for acquiring intelligence and managing crises are presented by developments in artificial intelligence, quantum computing, and space-based monitoring. The Situation Room's ability to remain effective in the face of changing threats will depend on how well these technologies are integrated into its operations.

By looking ahead

readers obtain a thorough grasp of the possibilities and difficulties that will influence the Situation Room's functioning in the years to come. The chapter emphasizes how crucial it is to preserve national security through ongoing innovation, strategic foresight, and adaptable leadership.

Conclusion
Reflections and Insights

In conclusion, the Situation Room is evidence of the US government's tenacity, flexibility, and strategic thinking. The Situation Room has changed throughout the years in response to the needs of contemporary crisis management and the shifting global environment, from its beginnings in the early 1960s to its current position at the center of national security.

The rich history of the Situation Room has been examined in this book, with particular attention paid to significant individuals, historical crises, and contemporary issues that have shaped its functioning. We have explored the moral conundrums, technical developments, and media dynamics that influence the decision-making process, providing a thorough grasp of the intricacies and obligations of individuals who occupy this crucial place.

The value of making well-informed decisions, conducting thorough analyses, and employing flexible tactics is shown by historical experiences, both triumphant and unsuccessful. The Situation Room needs to stay at the vanguard of national security as the world changes, utilizing cutting-edge techniques and new technologies to counter new threats.

In the end, the Situation Room represents American resolve and serves as a beacon of strategic leadership in addition to being a physical location. This book's comments and insights help readers gain a greater understanding of the struggles and victories that characterize the Situation Room's operations and the ongoing dedication to preserving national security.

NOTE

NOTE

NOTE